Photography by:
Jane Goodall, Derek Briceson,
M. Owens, Michael Neugebauer.

BABOON FAMILY
Jane Goodall

A MADISON MINI BOOK

Published by Madison Marketing Limited.
Madison Marketing Limited holds the exclusive
license to this edition.
Copyright © 1991 by Neugebauer Rights & Licenses AG., Zurich.
Text copyright © 1991 by Jane Goodall.
All rights reserved.
ISBN 1-55066-019-5

Printed in Canada

Printed on recycled paper

BABOON
FAMILY
Jane Goodall
ANIMAL SERIES

*P*hotographs selected by
Michael Neugebauer

/\/\

Madison Marketing Limited

*P*umpkin is three months old. His mother, Petal, is about 25 years old. She is quite old for a baboon. Pumpkin will probably be her last baby.

Pumpkin is full of energy, and loves to play with the other young baboons in his troop. He spends most of his time with his three year old sister, Poppy, and his cousin, Plum.

Pumpkin has five older brothers and sisters, four aunts and seven cousins. All the members of his family have names that begin with "P". There are six other big families in the troop of 52 baboons. Each family has names that begin with a different letter.

There are also eight big males in the troop. They don't belong to any of the seven families. When a young male is about 10 years old, ready to be a father, he leaves his family and moves into a different troop. Pumpkin has never met his two oldest brothers. They left the troop before he was born.

When the baboons wake up they sit around in the early morning sunshine and the males and females groom each other. Females will groom other females, but males never groom other males.

The young ones play while the adults are grooming. A chimpanzee family passes by and a young female stops for a quick game with her baboon friend.

When the troop sets off to search for food, the infants ride on their mothers. The tiny babies cling underneath. The older ones ride on top.

Soon they arrive at a grove of trees where there is plenty of food. Some of the baboons eat fruit. Others eat tender leaves. They like some kinds of insects, too, and even meat.

Pumpkin chews on a bright red palm nut. He is only playing. Since he's still so young, he usually just drinks his mother's milk.

The troop moves to a sandy beach on the shores of Lake Tanganyika. The youngsters love to play on the beach. When the lake is calm they like to swim. The fishermen living here catch little fish at night, and spread them out to dry in the morning sun. The baboons try to steal the fish, but the fishermen chase them off. They can't hurt the baboons. This is a National Park where all the animals are protected.

Suddenly a great commotion starts. Two males begin to fight over a female. She is ready to start a baby, and both males want to be the father. While this is going on another male tries to run off with the female. There are baboons running and barking and screaming everywhere. Pumpkin and Plum and the other young ones all run to their mothers. Soon it is peaceful again. The winning male keeps his female away from the others.

When the young ones play lots of little squabbles break out. If Pumpkin gets into trouble, Poppy usually runs to help him. She will help little Plum as well.

The adult males are very protective of infants. And sometimes they use the infants to protect themselves. Jones is frightened that Henry will attack him, so he takes Pumpkin into his arms. Pumpkin thinks this is fun. Jones knows Henry won't attack him because Pumpkin might get hurt. But Pumpkin only feels safe in his mother's arms.

The baboons have been lucky today. It's the rainy season, and some days it pours and pours. But today has been dry. And now the troop is enjoying the soft sunshine of the late afternoon. Some are lying stretched out on the warm ground. There is much peaceful grooming. Pumpkin and his other young friends are, of course, still playing.

When Petal moves off, following the others towards the tall sleeping trees, Pumpkin bounces after her and climbs onto her back. It is almost dark when she climbs to her favorite place. She sits on a broad branch and leans against the trunk of a great tree. All around other baboons are settling down for the night. Pumpkin will sleep soundly tonight, secure in his mother's arms. Even if it rains, she will huddle over her son and he will stay warm and dry.

*J*ANE GOODALL has shared her important discoveries and her love of animals with millions of people around the world through books, films and lectures. She has founded ongoing research and educational institutes on two continents, and is one of the world's most acclaimed naturalists.

The Jane Goodall Institute for Wildlife
Research, Education and Conservation
P.O. Box 41720, Tucson, AZ 85717 U.S.A.

The Jane Goodall Institute — Canada
P.O. Box 3125, Station "C"
Ottawa, Ontario K1Y 4J4 Canada

The Jane Goodall Institute — U.K.
15 Clarendon Park
Lymington, Hants SO41 8AX United Kingdom

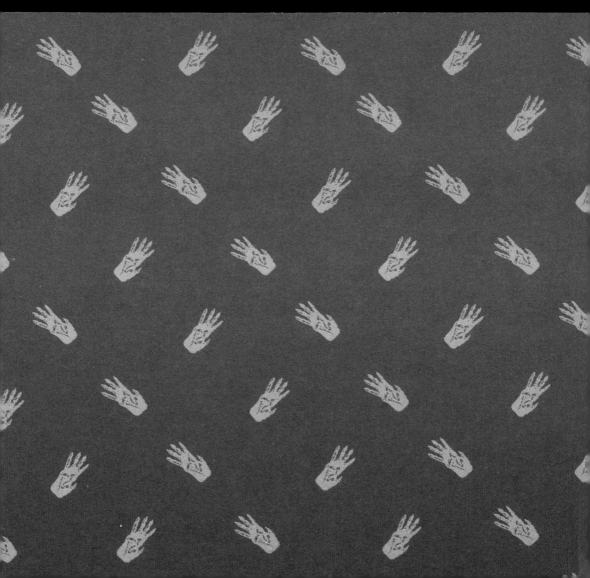